FSC
www.fsc.org
MIX
Papier aus verantwortungsvollen Quellen
Paper from responsible sources
FSC® C105338

PETE RUSSELL

MY PEN SAID IT

I hope that you will
enjoy this book!
Take care.
Pete

Dear reader,

I, as the publisher, may or may not agree with the content of this book, or parts of it, but it is and remains the unadulterated words of the author himself, edited as little as possible. I believe in freedom of speech and that the death penalty is wrong without any exception. There is a saying, "*You can tell the value of a society by how it treats the weakest of its members.*" I believe that to be true. That's why I give these members of society the opportunity to raise their voice. Most of them have undergone a transformation for the better. They have developed a mental strength in prison that we can't even imagine due to being locked up and forgotten about. Even after all these years they are still there; living, learning and rising beyond themselves. We can learn from them as much as they can learn from us. To silence one of them would be to silence all of us.

Stefan Heikens

Cover Design and Artwork: Stefan Heikens
Edited by: Mishelle Bushelle / Nicole Niehoff
Herstellung und Verlag: BoD – Books on Demand, Norderstedt
ISBN: 9783755737070

CONTENTS

INTRODUCTION

Our ancestors used poetry, more specifically spoken word poetry, to catalog our history; as well as use it as an apparatus to teach the next generation. In these rhythmic words there was triumph. These words, as well as the speaker, were triumphant because throughout everything - the pain, the joy and of course the embedment of a culture so rich, so resilient, it empowered each generation. Some may say without the rapture of those words and lessons a nation of people were lost. Poetry is emotions in rhythm, a tune of a life lived, where each note will bring another turn, another lesson, another fight. It's the irregular heartbeat inside a body trying so hard to navigate its way through its journey. Poetry is equivalent to that doctor informing you of clogged arteries: the inability of blood (life) to flow freely. Those rhythmic words diagnosing hypertension, indicating the ways of the world are indeed getting to you. It's the result of something you consumed with your ears, that your mind ate and digested out of your mouth; now forcing you to bring about action to those words in the form of disease. Pete Russell illustrates just how powerful an instrument held in one's hand, that is driven by the most powerful instrument known to man: the mind (more elaborately the third eye) can be. You will be able to feel exactly what his pen said as it captures social issues that have plagued this nation for so long, hindering our growth, especially our unity. More importantly, Mr. Russell's tune highlights his very own insight as to how the political forces affect and effect, both him and us all. To digest these words brings about a consciousness that has seemed to be lost in today's culture: To be an active participant as well as a harborer of the very thing that links us all together - humanity. It is my hope, as well as my good friend Pete Russell's hope, that this age-old method of spoken word brings us back full circle to the oneness that's essential to our evolution. Anyone with a heartbeat will definitely catch the tune of Mr. Russell and no doubt fall into his rhythm. Peace.

- Mabry J Landor III

Little Bitty Black Woman

She is only four feet tall!
The sister really surprised me because
she has been tricked into participating in sick cere-
monies and rituals.
Modern day lynchings that have been polished up
and served to the public.
I ask myself, do she understand what she is doing?

I see you Little Bitty Black Woman,
walking with a mob of whiteness.
Times have changed and so I write this.
Little Bitty Black Woman
you know that shit ain't righteous.

Little Bitty Black Woman
with your expensive clothes on.
Little Bitty Black Woman
why don't you go home?
Ms. BE-ALL-I-CAN-BE-IN-TDC.

Little Bitty Black Woman
they are going to kill me!
Little Bitty Black Woman
they are going to kill me.

Little Bitty Black Woman
you act like you don't hear me.
Little bitty Black woman
I know you don't fear me?
Little Bitty Black Woman with the

cell phone in your hand,
you smile, you giggle, you like "The Man".

Little Bitty Black Woman
do you understand?
Little Bitty Black Woman
I don't want to get in that van.
You know "The Man", you know his plans
and you're still shaking his hand.

Little Bitty SELLOUT!

Behind The Scenes

Like a bad dream, I was behind the scene. You should have seen it, the bullshit, the trickery, the hypocrisy. The feds tried to stop me from writing this poem, knowing that it would cause harm. For the movers and shakers, money makers, inside traders, corporate lawbreakers … The lying, cheating … Taxpayers suffer, crying and illing. The middle class bust they ass for dimes and nickels, sour politics, like kosher pickles … (Behind the scenes)

A team of men, fat cats like Goldman Sachs. Big wigs, greedy pigs, invaders on Wall Street. Who cheat and beat the people out of their money. To big to fail? I can't tell. Tricked into buying stocks with poison honey. Who plot and plan around the table with the Cain ... Nature, trying to kill Abel. Just throw me on the table. It's call the gurney in this journey.

A flat cross, the son of man, who is the boss, I pay the cost through the double cross. Never seen it coming like a blind fly in the web of injustice. Struggling against the weight of oppression. The mental impression recovered and stored in my subconscious. The attacks, the abuse, so many punches began to play out like a BP blowout.

The oil flow, like the blood flow, human flesh on the show. Room floor, politically whipped and shipped through the side door. 443 is my number and freedom is my hunger. Meditation is my secret.

I keep it in my heart every night. I depart one scene after another.

And you thought all the gambling went on in Vegas … Have you lost your mind? Do you know what it means to go behind the scenes? To see with your own eyes people sitting around a table. Trying to conspire how to rob Amerika blind. Knowing they want face time. Like Enron they want to run away with the money and stick you with the bill. You don't believe me? Go behind the scenes.

Can You Smell It?

Can you smell it?
Can you smell it?
Can you smell it?
I can!

I am seeking freedom, justice and equality, brothers and sistas holla at me. Brothers and sistas save me, liberate me from an unjust system that has plans to execute me for a crime / offense that I did not commit and the jury found me guilty ain't that some shit.

Can you smell it?
Can you smell it?
Can you smell it?
I can!

There is a toxic gumbo cooking here on the death row. Can you smell it? I can! The Polunsky Unit has become very funky in the way they treat us. The way they see us, the way they feed us. Mental abuse is the way they beat us. At the end of the day you should see us, looking crazy all doped up. Texas dummy, dead man walking. Call me the mummy.

Can you smell it?
Can you smell it?
Can you smell it?
I can!

There is a crisis going on right here in Texas and people are not paying attention to it. Like ‘Night of the living dead’. Perry is very scary, and Bush is burning candles. I got a spell on me. Mental warfare over health care. My name is Atkins. I got issues but they don't care. I need a sick call, and that's three dollars. No money on the books, make me wanna holla.

Can you smell it?

Inside My Cage

I am a 21st century slave born and raised in the
United States Of America.

Inside my cage the untold story,
projects and woodrats, youngsters and Cadillacs.
Swagging and banging
on the corner pants be hanging.

Inside my cage,
a menace to society,
please try me - armed and dangerous
running the streets with strangers.

Inside my cage,
a nobody trying to tell everybody
about somebody.
The black slave from the old days
the field nigga I refuse to behave.
I know why the caged bird sings.
Nobody knows the trouble I've seen.

Inside my cage,
I came to death row at a young age.
The young, the gifted and black
under attack by H.I.S.D.I.
was set up for T.D.C.
and Abraham Lincoln lied to me.

Inside my cage,
locked away 24 hours a day,

locked down and disrespected
like a modern day slave.
I suppress the black rage
pacing the floor at night
sweating like a hebrew slave.
Praying to god that everything will be alright.

Inside my cage,
I weigh my options
do I shank 'em, how do I stop them?
Bad dreams from a mad scene
Nightmares making inmates scream.

Inside my cage,
sometimes I am very optimistic,
but this is Texas and the politics are wicked.
And Governor Perry is trying to kill me
and the Supreme Court won't hear me.

Inside my cage,
I write this piece hoping you will feel me.
Shackles on my feet
and it's hard for me to kick it.
Bound and chained by the wicked.

Inside my cage,
I rebel against the beat
there will never be peace.
Sleep deprivation, can't get no sleep.

Inside my cage,
the black Shakespeares from the African hemisphere,
wise poetry from deep within.
Brothers and sisters we are bound to win
the hearts and minds of the people,
if you love the truth accept the sequel.

I stand on my bunk and scream
"Power to the people!“
Black, White and Brown!
We are all equal!
Inside my cage.

Shaking Hands

As I look out my window,
into a world of symbolism, rituals
and ceremonies;
prepare yourself for my testimony,
see through my eyes,
don't hate on me.

The old school, the new school,
the old school, the new school.

The southern man, the Klu Klux Klan man,
the real boys in the hood.
Kill a brother man!
The real boys in the hood,
kill a brother man.

I can see them from my window.
shaking hands, coming from the hip
with secret grips.
I repeat!
Shaking hands, coming from the hip
With secret grips … FreeMason.

The old school, the new school,
the old school, the new school.

OJTS's and new boots with confederate
gray suites, and shiny boots.
OJTS's and new boots with confederate
gray suites, and shiny boots.

Skinning and grinning, breath stinking,
beer drinking, I wonder what
the hell they thinking?

Shaking hands, clapping hands,
shaking hands, clapping hands.

12 o'clock on the dot,
we have a dead man,
from visitation to
the white van.
Who's behind the wheel - a bad man.
And these are the facts,
no need to trip,
watch the hands of the Klan,
coming from the hip.

Shaking Hands – Pt. II

Smiling foxes surround him
paws stained of morbid blood
poison subtly enters him
metallic death fills his lungs.

Your chariot awaits.

Forced through those wide gates
you pray for a stay while they
celebrate you as prey.

He is in.

Smiling faces from death graces
looks at the joyous occasion
murdering every month,
but swear you're shedding the death rating.

Hands shake.

Saintly facades over devilish objectives.
Masking murders behind legal documents,
ya'll shaking hands for the stayings
with no humility.

What happened to the civility?

Shaking Hands 3:0
Alto The Graceful Gazelle

The lion of life chased the gazelle,
once caught wanted to save him from hell.
Until he heard laughing, peering in the distance,
he sees the pack of hyenas lurking smirking.
Knowing they have their kill,
the lion of life has lost his Gazelle.

The hyenas surround their prey
and sink their needle like teeth in.
Poison from the scavenger flow
and the gazelle lays still.

Another casualty to this vicious jungle,
the vicious jungle we call justice.
The hyenas shake hands and smile,
"We will laugh together next week".

The lion of life has lost again,
Alto the graceful Gazelle becomes the victim.
The victim of the Hyenas
called the administration.

R.I.P. Beunka Adams

Texas Kill

Hurry, hurry, hurry.
Hurry, hurry, hurry.
Hurry, hurry, hurry.

Step right up. Step right up. Step right up, come on brother - Step right up. Step right up. Don't be afraid.

To the greatest lynching of all times, the Texas killing machine, the penal Frankenstein.

Hundred years of killing, Banjo playing, tobacco spitting, dirty dealing from the old country folks.

Leave it to Beaver, back in the day the trail ride, the hayride. Caveman you need to behave man. Hillbillys barefoot and hooded, moonshine drinking. Billy Bob with no job. Killing to pass time, cracking jokes. People protest, no justice, no peace, stop the killing. Houston Chronicle the 5th circuit is the beast. 'Nightmare On Elm Street' was fiction, but here in Huntsville it's the religion, and Buddah keeps killing me with sad songs of Dixie.

Hurry, hurry, hurry.
Hurry, hurry, hurry.
Hurry, hurry, hurry.
Step right up, step right up.
Come one, come all.
Come one, come all.
Big, fat and tall.
Christian man, christian woman.
Christian man, christian woman.

Bring your bible
let's have revival.

Slave obey your master. Come here you black bastard to get the greatest lynching of all times. The Texas killing machine, the penal Frankenstein.

Look close, understand the deal, understand the history of how Texas kills. The anti lynching bill justice carried out in a cornfield. See the contradiction? My judge dyed his robe black to hide white magic. 'Harry Potter', we ain't having it. A group of wicked 'masons. From Harris County to the wall's plantation, mama at home singing songs for her sins of salvation.

Hurry, hurry, hurry.
Hurry, hurry, hurry.
Hurry, hurry, hurry.
Step right up, step right up.
Step right up, step right up.
Hurry, hurry, hurry.
To the greatest lynching of all times,
the Texas killing machine, the penal Frankenstein.

Today is a great day to be alive. So I continue the struggle to stay alive. But great is the temptation to break free and find salvation. I do it through meditation, it's the only reparation for mental peace. From the slave plantation to get away from Polunsky. A five man team trying to punk me. They pray that I die and rough me up. Push me in the van for a good ole boy ride. License expired doing zero to sixty. We got this trigger, we kill him tonight and all my people continue to fight.

J.A.G.

The Journey, the Attorney, the Gurney.
The Journey, the Attorney, the Gurney.
The Journey, the Attorney, the Gurney.

The Journey begins without friends, all alone without sin … the fetal position. Tossing and turning acid reflux burning nine months in the womb, a child is born within a world of doom. Innocent child, innocent smile and rippin' and running. How many miles? Dark journey never seen the gurney.

The Journey, the Attorney, the Gurney.
The Journey, the Attorney, the Gurney.
The Journey, the Attorney, the Gurney.

The Attorney comes in, stretched out arms, rolex watch! Bling! Blind to the game. So I never watch the grin of justice blazing across his face. Dumb to the game as he takes my case. Reality sets in, I don't like this place. I take the stand and tell the truth the jury came back and gave me the boot. GUILTY!

The Journey, the Attorney, the Gurney.
The Journey, the Attorney, the Gurney.
The Journey, the Attorney, the Gurney.

I find myself, by myself. From the beginning, searching for self - locked away in a small filthy cage - staring out the window looking at the stars, can't help but see the bars. Could this be hell?

The devil would never tell something is wrong. I'm a long way from home. The knife of injustice slowly cuts as brothers are led away in chains and cuffs. The white van backs up vroooom, vrooooom. I have heard that song before, chains dragging the floor, screaming at the top of my lungs. Please Lord, not no more. Is this the meaning of my journey? Will it end on the Gurney? I look around, where is my Attorney?

The Journey, the Attorney, the Gurney.
The Journey, the Attorney, the Gurney.
The Journey, the Attorney, the Gurney.

What Do You Do?

What do you do my brother when they come for you?
What do you do my brother when they come for you?
What do you do my brother when they come for you?

Do you cop out or cop in?
Do you run / do you hide?
Do you freeze up / bitch up?
Panic and commit suicide?
Do you lie?
Do you cheat?
Do you steal?
Do you go behind the scenes and cut deals?
Do you vote?
Do you smoke?
Do you march?
Do you sing?
Do you swing?

What do you do my brother when they come for you?
What do you do my brother when they come for you?
What do you do my brother when they come for you?

Do you know the man?
Do you talk to the man?

Do you shake his hand?
Do he has your back?
Do you scratch his back?
Do you get down like that?
Do you Uncle Tom?
Do you Uncle Sam?
Do you go crazy?
Do you say GOT DAMN?
Do you shut up?
Do you speak up?
Do you take a stand?
Do you strap up?

What do you do my brother when they come for you?
What do you do my brother when they come for you?
What do you do my brother when they come for you?

Do you A.K.?
Do you banana clip?
Are you mad?
Do you let it rip? (pop.pop.pop.)

What do you do my brother when they come for you?
What do you do my brother when they come for you?
What do you do my brother when they come for you?

Do you like the 9?
Do you understand the time?
Do you know what it means when I say "red, black and green"?
Do you know Mr. AR-15?
Did you know I had guerillas on my team?

What do you do my brother when they come for you?
What do you do my brother when they come for you?
What do you do my brother when they come for you?

Devil 21

9 dead …
Now he lay us down
for our final sleep,
as Negros weep.

White Judas -
Mr. Blue eyes,
please don't shoot us.

Born out of a poison womb into a sick society, just trying to be a good Christian. My third eye was closed, so I missed him.

We let the devil in hoping we could be friends. We smiled and he grinned, overlooking his blue eyes. I should have realized that devil 21 was up to no good. Drove over 200 miles just to get to the hood. We let him in, the church said AMEN.

9 dead …
Now he lay us down
for our final sleep,
as Negros weep.

White Judas -
Mr. Blue eyes,
please don't shoot us.

We study the book every Wednesday night. I never knew tonight would be our last. Shame on me for overlooking Mr. Blue eyes. Goose bumps on my arms as we read the 23rd psalm: "Yeah though I walk through the valley of the shadow of death, I will fear no evil".

We opened our eyes and to our surprise devil 21 had a gun. Born out of a poisoned womb into a sick society, a high school drop-out dropped in with a heart full of sin. Just trying to be a good Christian, my third eye was closed so I missed him.

Pop, pop, pop, pop, pop, pop, pop, pop, pop, pop

9 dead …
Now he lay us down
for our final sleep,
as Negros weep.

White Judas -
Mr. Blue eyes,
please don't shoot us.

Mr. Fears

My name is Mr. Fears and I too shed tears. I have been down for many many years.

Sometimes I can't take it. The pressure becomes so great, I touch things and they break!

There is a death row syndrome with psychological effects. Stressing people out, beating down the walls trying to get out.

I don't know who will be next in this prison industrial complex. No disrespect but suicide is hard to detect.

I am isolated and the story I tell seems complicated. Just trying to remain alive in a dead system. I shed tears cuz I miss him …

R.I.P. Tony/Tone

The Blind World

They continue to stare death in the face with blind eyes. Poison animal eaters, they become not knowing the time or the hour. Slowly dying off like shit eating flies. Death is breathing down their necks, will they ever wake up and realize?

Wake Up

Let those who have ears …
Let them hear …
The only thing that's real … is that needle in
Huntsville … wake up and chill.
The state of Texas is killing us left and right …

And what do you do?
You gossip and shoot kites.
You gossip and shoot kites.

He said / she said
I don't mess with him.
He said / she said
I don't pass for him.
He said / she said,
he jacked me for my kite.
He said / she said,
one potato, two potato.
The state of Texas is killing us left and right …

And what do you do?
You gossip and shoot kites.
You gossip and shoot kites.

A Sick Portrait

I paint this picture for those people in the free world, who are sincerely enquiring about the mental health and physical conditions here on Texas death row. Where people check in and most of the time we are rolled out dead! God will take us home. A mother's tears reflect the years not being able to kiss her son.

What is wrong with this picture?

I am forced to paint this picture without traditional brush, emotion building up, about to erupt on a mental canvas of madness. Each stroke depicting the empty space of an empty mind, the colors I use are color blind. They have lost their minds, even the mind thinks he is crazy, leave mine alone!

What is wrong with this picture?

They stand at the door waiting on the store knowing that they don't have no money. Waiting on a bag they've never seen or had, only increases the mad. Sometimes they are psyched out standing at the door trying to explore the big world with eyes closed, describing things they've never seen, like a baby drooling at the mouth. Heavenly medicated with K.O.P.'s - while rubbing feces on his skin. I wonder do he has friends? The death row syndrome won't leave them alone.

Afrikan Drum

Master Charlie took my drum away from me.
Can you believe that?
Said he didn't like the sound of my beat.
Said he didn't like the way I patted my feet.
Said he didn't like the way I shake my hand.
Poor Master Charlie.

We just laugh, we just laugh, we just laugh.

Master Charlie took my drum away from me.
I guess Master Charlie thinks I'm weak.
Now Master Charlie can't sleep.
Now Master Charlie can't eat.
Poor Master Charlie … what did y'all do?
Nothing!

We laugh, we just laugh, we just laugh.

Master Charlie took my drum away from me.
They say Master Charlie is sick.
They say Master Charlie don't have long to live.
They say Master Charlie was foaming at the mouth.
Said he took ill.
Did you see his wife's tears?
Poor Master Charlie.

We just laugh, we just laugh, we just laugh.

Master Charlie took my drum away from me.
They say Master Charlie done lost his mind.

People say Master Charlie have committed a bad, bad crime.
Said he killed his wife and kids after drinking a bottle of bad, bad wine … What!
Poor Master Charlie.

We just laugh, we just laugh, we just laugh.

Black Folks

They don't believe the signs of the time.
They don't believe 60,000 years of crime.
They are still living in denial.
They're blood will flow like the Nile.
They have turned their backs on history.
They never understand the mystery.

Congo Red

There is a holocaust in the Congo and the river flows red.

There is a holocaust in the Congo and the river flows red.

Over ten million died and the ancestors cried. When will we get justice from those who trample us?

Where is the UN? I thought we were friends. When will they stop raping our country? Has anyone seen my gold they stole? Has anyone seen King Leopold? Can you tell him to send back my rubber. He fooled me, I thought we were brothers.

Dope Fiend

Around the clock, he walks up and down,
to and fro, throughout the streets of America.

Through rain, sleet and snow,
blowing his nose with Cali Coke,
as he enjoys his trip and cloud nine.

The Newport cigarette hangs from his cracked lips,
struggling hard to maintain his habit,
out of control dope fiend picks up bad habits.

Dope fiend steals - He'll grab it,
have you seen my lawnmower?

Ghetto Memories

I am a 1973 baby, old school my Mama raised me.
I have been around the block
with holes in my socks.
Dope dumped in my hood
So I opened up shop.
Thanks to the C.I.A. - niggas bleed the block.

Never seen my Pops,
at an early age running from the cops.
Mom is working 9-5
I'm in the jungle trying to survive.
Untamed Gorilla with bananas clips
I never bang, but I know Crips,
I never bang, but I know Crips.

My resident is unamerican,
good times, and bad times.
Bombed out like Iraq,
do you have my back?
No justice for none of us.

Locked down on Gitmo-Prophey with Moto.
My background is ghetto,
like South Africa, Soweto.
Now I am here in America,
and to tell you the truth
I am scared of her.
I don't want the Statue Of Liberty,
the bitch is trying to kill me!

Mental Illness

Mental illness is spreading like wildfire across America and so I pray: Lord please, save your children from mental illness.

Lord please save your children from mental illness.

The nightmares, the cold sweats, the shakes, the shivers. My brother with the bad liver, too much to drink, bootleg and bad liquor rot gut, and corn liquor too.

Lord please save your children from mental illness.

What's wrong with my dome? I try to do right, but I find myself doing wrong.

Lord please save your children from mental illness.

The K-2 smoker, the local joker, the straight jacket, the straight shooter. Homeless people and desperate looters.

Lord please save your children from mental illness.

The despies and the rejected, home alone babies, bad mothers - child neglected. The crackhead, the meth head, the geeker and tweaker. Tom, Dick and Harry and pedophile preachers.

Lord save your children from mental illness.

The pharmaceutical company, experimental drugs. Kids with down syndrome looking for hugs. Big brother and satellites, invisible laser beams, brain-washed white kids picking up AR-15s.

Lord please save your children from mental illness.

From the suicide bomber, I pray he don't harm us. Save us from fake news and Fox news, save us from Mr. Trump, and Putin. Save us from the brothers on the block that be shootin'.

Lord please save your children from mental illness.

Amen …

My Noisy Neighbor

Like clockwork they
drop packs of pills off
and when nighttime comes,
I can hear him going off.

My noisy neighbor is really not to blame.
Some say mental illness
but who I am to complain?
My noisy neighbor is off the chain,
but with patience and perseverance
I remain sane.

Routine Dehumanization

While you're at home enjoying life,
kick back and relax,
not a worry in the world
whatsoever.
There is a system in place that
takes pride in destroying human beings.
A system designed to break the will and mind.

Forgot about, we the people.
Forgot about, post racial America.
Forgot about, vote for me!
Forgot about, man was created
in the image of God.

Understand the system on a daily basis.
Continue the process of elimination,
by routinely dehumanizing individuals
that are incarcerated.
Let me give you an example of a sadistic ritual
that takes place everyday across America.

What if I told you to take off your clothes?
Take off the damn shoes too!
What if I told you to raise your hands in the air?
No you are not under arrest … just do what I say.
What if I told you to run your fingers through your
hair?
By the way, you need a haircut too.
What if I told you to open your mouth and stick out
your tongue?

Just say "aaaaaaaaaa" and wiggle your tongue.
What if I told you to lift your feet up?
Come on now, you can do it, one foot at a time.
What if I told you to lift your nutz up?
What if I told you to turn around and spread your cheeks?
You heard me … open your ass boy!
Say what?!
Inmate are you disobeying an order?
Fuck you! I am a man, not an animal.
"Gas that nigger" - *SHHHHHHH*, *SHHHHHHHHHHH*, *cough*, *cough*, *cough*.
I am a man! I am a man!
SHHHHHHH...*SHHHHH*
You will be a dead man, when I finish with you…*SHHHHHH*

Inmate found dead in his cell.
He stood as a man.
He had a right to rebel.
But the prison will never tell.

Run!

Run! Run! Run!
You can't escape me.
You can't hide from me.
You need me.

How else can you cope in America?
Your dream is my nightmare
and this is your brain on drugs.

Run! Run! Run!
Just run!
Look at you
you are jobless.
Homeless.
Hopeless with no benefits.

That's right, throw up your hands and
Run! Run! Run!
Just run!

You can't escape me.
You can't hide from me.
I have been allowed to consume you wholesale.
You claim you hate drugs,
but when night time comes you embrace me with a hug.
You say you hate smoking crack,
but when night time comes you are sucking on my pipe.
You tell your friends that you are afraid of heights,

but when night time comes you're higher than a kite.

Run! Run! Run!
Just run!
How else can you cope in Amerika?
I have been allowed to consume you wholesale.
This is not a war against drugs,
this is a war against you.
Reflect on this truth,
and maybe then you'll kick the habit.
Until then just
Run! Run! Run!
Just run!

Sad Memories

I was told I was an endangered species,
the last of a dying breed.
A.U.F.O brotha et brotha.
Divine god Osiris,
lord of the perfect black melanin covered.

Invaded by the other
Europeans with wicked schemes,
kidnapped and chained from the mother.
Cultural gang bang,
disconnected from my brother.
Never had a chance to say goodbye,
my family was split and so I cried.

The slave trade,
on the ship of Jesus.
The slave trade,
I was whipped on Jesus.
The slave trade,
I lost my mind on Jesus.
Played like a game of spades
and these are sad memories.

Suicide

Suicidal thoughts, rise and fall,
they pop in and out
affecting us all.
Taking shape in the cracks and crevices of the mind.
Bad dreams, and nightmares,
demonic screams and laughter.
Dirty demons dancing under a full moon.
Taunting me,
I am paralysed,
horrified, I can't move.
A distant voice screams:
Russsell, are you eating?
Yes … Yes.

Terrorism

The manufactured boogie man,
created by a stroke of the pen.
The man who never was, but a wizard!
Pale hands with evil plans
dropping bombs on the holy land.

Smoke and mirrors
and the truth is on the wall.
Read it! Read it!
A false flag operation,
9-11 what's your emergency?

The Chair

Eighty four percent of Texans sentenced to the electric chair between 1924 and 1928 were African American. Of the forty five Texans who died in the electric chair, seven were white, four of Mexican descent and thirty four were African American.

We arrived at the Huntsville Museum like a thief in the night. It was raining cats and dogs. It was me and chaplain. We came to say goodbye to old Sparky.

I sneak in with my friend, so that he can watch my back. The chaplain hands me the axe. I raise the big axe high up into the air. The chaplain smiles.

HURRY UP BROTHER - DO IT NOW!

An act of justice, I must carry out. My adrenaline is rushing, beads of sweat dripping off my face, as the chaplain stares off into space. A silent prayer for both of us, I can see the expression on his face.

HURRY UP BROTHER - DO IT NOW!

The big axe hovering above my head as I reflect on the dead. The horror, the pain. Man was made in the image of God, only to be strapped down in the chair of injustice.

HURRY UP BROTHER - DO IT NOW!

I bring the axe down with all my might. BOOM! The museum seems to shake. I can hear the dead rejoicing in heaven as I chop away at history. Never again Sparky. Never again.

CHOP! CHOP! CHOP!

The Texas Holocaust

The Texas holocaust is one of many holocausts that continue to take place right here in Texas.

Believe it or not, this is not a mystery, but history manifesting right before your eyes.
Wake up people before it's too late or someone else might die.

A first class ticket from the hood to the death house.
Poor inmates are dying because they couldn't afford the cost of a good attorney.
And many of us are strapped to the gurney with poison needles in our arms, closed eyes.

Reciting psalms, a modern day crucifixion had action on appeal and Clarence Thomas is tripping.
The lone star state - the human slaughterhouse.

See we (politicians) kill for the thrill
like Jack and Jill you want to see an inmate on boot hill,
penitentiary funeral home,
I say no deal.

Six feet deep body cold as steel...
I don't want no last meal.
I want justice brother - you say no deal, cruel and unusual punishment.

It's the heart beat of Texas and inmates feel the
brunt of it.

Texas history from the noose to the needle ain't no
mystery.
Lord please save me!
In 2018 it seems like slavery.

This Cell

This cell is that cell
and that cell is this cell,
Every six months they move us from cell to cell.

And you never know about your cell,
until you enter the cell.
Who was in my cell?
What is that cell?
Do this cell leaks?
My God this cell stinks!
What is that on my cell floor?
Could it be a puddle of urine from a pissed off in-
mate?

And back to that smell.
Could it be human feces
placed on the side of the bunk?
Out of sight, out of mind?
But I smell that shit!

White Lines

Not the kind you sniff, snort or toot,
but the kind you see up in the sky.
Pay close attention and realize
White lines better known as chemtrails.
Trails of poison slowly falling down on us,
a grid is sprayed in the sky.
Blowing your minds, causing health problems,
you will see long white lines coming from the jet.
Some people call these lines fairydust,
or cotton candy.
They expand as they fall … they look like clouds,
white lines is a global affair.
Look up!

325 A.D.

We wear the mask of Christianity.
To fool humanity.
Our killing spree reveals our insanity.

Breaking News

Pedophile priest molesting little boys
Porno tapes and sex toys
Dildos and buttballs
Magic tricks and joysticks.

Used and abused performing Black Mass
lusting on little Johnny's ass.
Behind closed doors with no clothes on
sipping on Jesus Juice feeling tipsy.
Reading out the book of John
Having fun.

Baptized in dirty water
Traumatized kids sing the blues
Like Muddy Waters,
grown men broken inside.

Mary don't you weep
And Martha don't you moan
And Jesus wept too!

Crash Dummy

I was radicalized by Uncle Sam
I dropped out of school
I didn't give a damn.
I was hypnotize by the red, white and blue
Looking at his eyes he said:
I want you.

I signed up and I was ready for boot camp.
They gave me a gun
I was really amped,
they taught me how to fight and kill
six month later I was in the field.

Bombs were dropping and women were crying
America was losing and we were dying.
A Vietnamese man held his hand out
I was surrounded by enemies
I couldn't get out.

He gave me a note and told me to read
"Black Man go home this is not your war"
That's when I knew the joke was on me
Crush Dummy.

Crazy Man

Please don't stare at me.
They tease me, they taunt me.
I struggle to stay strong.
As reckless eyeballs cut me.
You see … they say I'm crazy
but this is the way God made me.
Some even front on me,
it's okay, I can handle it.

They say I am weird,
but it's simple math,
because everything adds up right?
They don't see what I see
they didn't read the books I read.
They don't move like me
and that's why I remain
free mentally!

Double Standard

If you sell a machine gun to a man,
and the gunman shoots several innocent people
then that man will be in a big trouble
and more than likely
you would get into trouble too.

But if America sells Saudi Arabia
one hundred billion dollars
worth of "Weapons Of Mass Destruction".
And the Saudi's use them against Yemen,
killing over ten thousand people,
mostly women and kids.
Nothing will happen to the King and his Son
and the oil will continue to flow …
Politics!

Fatherless

Have you seen my daddy?
I grew up in a single parent home all alone without a daddy.
Every now and then he would
Swing through in his sister's caddy playing games like.
WHO IS YOUR DADDY?

I was poor and didn't know it
Mama was struggling and he knew it.
Sent me books on Jehovah Witness
I was young, wax in my ear.
I wasn't listening.

Out of sight, out of mind
Emotional cuts here and there
Perpetrating the fraud
This negro didn't care
A sham of a man, acting nonchalant
fooling the family, they never had a hunch.

He comes and goes as he pleases
Like a cool breeze, in and out of my life.
His only son, abandoned me and Mom
For his barren wife.

Have you seen my daddy?

Hello

I pimp the pen on a daily.
As I write family and friends.
With greetings and solutions,
stimulating the mind,
reflecting on the good times,
as we meet each other in this sacred space.
Maintaining a harmonious friendship,
sprinkled with love and laughter.
As the black ink bleeds on the white paper.
Balancing our ying and yang.

IMF

The IMF is taxing Afrika to death
With high interest rates.
Corrupt leaders take money
and it's too late.
At the end of the day there's no food left on the people's plate.
Multi corporations raid the continent.
Like date rape.
While hungry people are screaming
Wait! Wait!

Inquiry

1. Did Trump get a 'golden shower' behind closed doors? Did Russia give him power? Did he ever build his tower?
2. Sarah Palin can see Russia from Alaska. Did she see Trump having sex with prostitutes? Just ask her.
3. Did she see Trump tap dancing in the palm of Putin's hands? Shaking his orange ass like only he can.
4. Do you think that's fake news? Indictments are coming and people will sing the blues, Michael Cohen!
5. Did Stormy Daniels have sex with Trump? Did she spank him on his orange rump? Did she use a time magazine? Can you picture that scene? Yuck!

Little Tommy

He was molested when he was a little boy.

Little Tommy's Mother's friend came over to party, smoke weed and drink gin. Somebody had eyes for little Tommy, gave him lots of candy and rubbed his tummy.

He was molested when he was a little boy.

They played with him like a little toy, dressed him up in little girl clothes.He was only seven years old. The hurt and pain is internalized scared for life with family lies. Someone spiked the punch and gave Tommy a sip or two took advantage of him that's what molesters do. A broken wrist with a southern twist. And you say "Who did this?"

He was molested when he was a little boy.

Me Too!

Can you buy me a drink?
Sure.
What would you have?
Sex on the beach....
What?!
You want to have sex with me?
You Creep! Get away from me…

Ladies and gentlemen, playing games
pointing the finger at each other.
Who is to blame?
He said - she said it was all the same.

Be a man, be a woman
accept responsibility.
Just tell the truth
and stop acting silly.
Keep your hands to yourself
and watch what you drink
and remember Hollywood
Is not what you think.

Planned Parenthood

God: Be fruitful and multiply.
Government: I don't think so,
they are in the hood up to no good
waiting to kill Mary's baby.

Medical mad scientist,
bloody needles and fetuses.
Mary is scared, but the baby is dead
body parts - like auto parts,
Stem cells - like record sales,
put the pieces together.

In fear of a Black planet,
and this is why they plan it
in the hood

DAMMIT!!!

Preacher Man

Let the church say amen - amen!
Preacher man.
Preacher man.
I never have seen a bible in his hand,
even though he believes in 'The Man'.

Sometimes he is drunk in spirit
uplifted, detached from the row.
Even I couldn't hear it.
Power walking, Power talking, bible thumping.

As he zooms freely around the dayroom
without a worry in the world.
Heart pumping, as salty sweat
drips from his black skin
while angels admire
and demons grin.
Preacher man.
Preacher man.

The Dayroom

This is not my first rodeo,
we kick back and relax.
Drinking speedball coffee,
crushed up cold busters
Spiked up coffee.

Cracking jokes laughing,
just to keep from crying.
Reminisce about the street life;
the money, the cars, and clothes.
Running from the law, kicking in doors.
At the club tricking off money with hoes.
Abandoned houses become Trap Houses.

Blowing trees and cats be flossy … Clean!
Blowing trees and cats be bossy … Shot callers!
Blowing trees and cats be dipping … Water!
Blowing trees and cats be tripping … Butt naked!
Blowing trees and cats be sipping … Purple stuff!
Blowing trees and this brother here
is sooooo high!
Sad!

We kick stories like these, passing time,
shooting the breeze
just you and me
in the dayroom.

The Walking Dead

I seen him with my own two eyes.
I seen him with my own two eyes.
I was in B - dayroom early in the morning August 21 2017.

It wasn't a dream.
I am telling you what I seen.
I seen him with my own two eyes.
I seen him with my own two eyes.

Walking slowly to the shower barefooted.
No shower shoes on.
His eyes were open, but he was already gone.
His eyes were open, but he was already gone.

I seen him with my own two eyes.
I thought to myself: is he still alive?
I seen him with my own two eyes.
I seen him with my own two eyes.

August 21 2017 it wasn't a dream,
I am telling you what I seen.
The walking dead, the walking dead.
The second shift came on,
I learnt that the inmate I seen had taken his life
and to make matters worse it was his birthday.

August 21, 2017, it wasn't a dream.
I am telling you what I seen.
The walking dead.

A Strong Mama

My mama is your mama
On the front line holding signs
Through rain, sleet and snow,
down in Huntsville where the
Killing is real.

Scream pen!
Scream pen!

A strong mama.
A black mama.
A white mama.
A brown mama.

High blood pressure,
Under pressure.

Wheel chairs, crutches and canes
Bad back, bad knees.
Mama in pain.

Scream pen!
Scream pen!

The young mama.
The old mama.
The struggling mama.
Work too hard mama.
A proud mama.

Scream pen!
Scream pen!

My mama is your mama.
Through thick and thin.
Pointing out sins of those
who worship the jinn.

Scream pen!
Scream pen!

Ritual killing.
Bone chilling.
Politicians giggling.
Praying for a stay.
Hoping to visit mama.
The next day, smile.

Scream pen!
Scream pen!

The death row angels are no strangers.
Been there, done that.
Righteous anger.
Raw and uncut.
Facebook live.
The world must know.
The world must rise.

Scream pen!
Scream pen!

Bad Daddy

Pete Jr.
Look at cha!
You just like your daddy.
Sorry! No good! Lazy!
No job … Look at cha!
(Only five years old).

Blind

The American people are blind and can't see.
Worried about brown skin people across seas.
All along the bear was grooming Agent Orange to take the White house.
And now the people are in the street screaming get out!

Confused

Mama dressed me in
Hand me down clothes.
Sent me off to school
with a sack lunch.
Do I stay in school?
I don't want to be nobody's fool.
Or do I stay in school and allow them to
prepare me for prison?
… Look at my report card!

Covid Rising

Cities, states and countries are locking down,
This is only the first round.
You would like to go back to school,
but don't be fooled.

You would like to go back to work
to overcome the economic hurt.
But all these things come with a price,
and what they have in store for us
won’t be nice.
BEWARE!

George Floyd

On the streets of Amerika;
I can’t breathe, I can’t breathe.

George Floyd was crucified and the whole world cried;
I can't breathe, I can't breathe.

George Floyd was crucified and the whole world riots;
I can't breathe, I can't breathe.

George Floyd was crucified and the whole world died with him;
I can’t breathe, I can’t breathe.

George Floyd was crucified under the ugly knee of racism.
By a crooked cop.
As innocent bystanders pleaded for big George Floyd’s life.
Right here, on the streets of Amerika.

Hack

Around the clock,
non stop
they are watching you.
The alphabet boys with sophisticated toys
hacking into your IPhone,
spying on you.
Turning your camera off and on
next it will be you
remote control.

House Call

The angel of death
Creeps in my cell
holding an hourglass,
pointing with his boney finger
at the sands of time.
Making me realize that
life is too short.

Lucky

I was shot in the leg.
Mama thought I was dead.
Thank god the bullet missed my head.
You can say I have 9 lives.
I am blessed to still be alive.
You grin but it's not funny.
I live in a war zone - “Fifth Ward”.

Made In America

I was told to pull myself up by my bootstraps,
if i wanted to experience the American dream.
Now the only boots I wear are made in Beijing.

Missing

Daddy burnt rubber on me and mama -
Like an illegal drag race.
Left us in the wind,
dust in our face.
Broken heart - broken home.
Lots of questions; daddy gone.

Nephew

You said you like Dizzy Gillespie
and John Coltrane
Then pick up your horn
and do your thang.
The world is yours
pick up your horn and blow!
Blow your horn Tra,
blow your horn.

Pickle Head

My homeboy is very disrespectful.
From his filthy mouth flies
"Bitches and hoes",
sprinkled with "fuck yous" too.
A dysfunctional family
between mother and son
But in the end, it's all love,
come on man …

Pic-Nic

I am not talking about family and food.
I am not talking about fun and games.
I am talking about the other Pic-Nic.

Just pick any nigga.
A tradition in America.
The execution of George Floyd was a modern day lynching.

Rhetoric

The Republicans and Democrats are reading from the same playbook,
trying to get elected using hook and crook.

Vote for me and I will set you free!

Two wings on the same bird, have you heard?

Look!
Up in the sky,
Is it a bird?
Is it a plane?
No, it's a shame!

Political theater at its best.
Behind closed doors who knows?
Rhetoric.

Sad Christmas

Christmas lights from a distance
as I sing jingle bells in my cell.
But the officer's walkie talkie tells another tale -
suicide before christmas, "F Pod".

Sanction

Uncle Sam is full of surprises,
third world countries don't realize this.
Playing games with funny money
printed out of thin air,
it will get you nowhere.
Dept slavery!

Southern Strategy

We have the Ingredients:

Take poor white people.
2 cans of misinformation.
Falsehood.

Shake very well.

Now whisper poison in their ears.
Magnify their fears and watch them go crazy
attacking Blacks and Mexicans.

For what?

American foreign policy in the form of domestic terrorists,
spilling out on Mainstreet.

The Next Wave

Next year will bring new fears,
mixed with champagne and tears.
Watch what they do in 2022
coming to a city near you.

Same game, new name.
Talking heads, people scared
people are falling in line.
No question asked!

People are losing their minds, side effects.
People are sticking out their arms,
waiting on a booster shot.
Six months later, you need a booster shot.
Coming to a city near you.
Same game, new name
Talking heads, people scared.

The Plot

Childhood memories over the years.
In silence, I plot with salty tears.
I plan, but I never execute a beat down.
She had it coming,
I buried my pain and kept moving.
I grew up.

The Set Up

Weapons of 'mass distraction' has caused inaction among the masses.

They never seen it coming behind the scenes pulling strings.
A human beings' worst nightmare;
shadows cast everywhere.

They groom you only to doom you,
slowly pushing you over the edge.
Come, come they say,
don't be scared

Big brother will catch you … Jump!
I know it's hard to believe.

What Is Love?

Love is the highest form of mathematics,
the foundation for family.
Love is U - N - I coming together.
In oneness manifesting the son of God,
the long awaited star child.

Whip Him

Post traumatic slave syndrome
runs deep in my home.
Tales from the whip!
Mama cried out:
Get that belt!
Get that belt!
The rage in her eyes and me in tears.
"No mama, no!"

Sometimes I would run and hide,
but most of the time
I obeyed her command.
From the womb I was groomed
To get that belt.

Battle Cry

Everyone on this planet is not asleep, trust me we are together and we have a plan. We are rising up around the world with one voice. In unison we are screaming:

My body, my choice!
My body, my choice!

We are a diverse movement, representing every culture under the sun. We are online, offline, off the chain, protesting and agitating in your face:

My body, my choice!
My body, my choice!

Either we stand up and fight the power, or let the power ensnare us. If we allow big brother to take away our voice, then we surrender everything I cluding the voiceless. A long as we have a voice we have a choice, and that's why we are screaming:

My body, my choice!
My body, my choice!

Black Power

After emancipation, fresh off the plantation, we were told to pull ourselves up by our bootstraps. What bootstraps?

Are you talking about the boots you wear to kick us around? The straps you use over and over to beat us down?

We didn't get the 40 acres, we didn't get the mule. And years later you dropped a bomb on move. So what do we do? We are going to seize the time, because the time is now!

It's about self determination. I don't know about you, but I am determined to do something for myself, for my people, my community and humanity as a whole. This is Black power and Black is beautiful.

Controversy 5.0

The New York Times called me controversy. Times magazine called me controversy. What is all this talk about controversy? No matter what I say or do, somebody is always calling me controversy.

When a person speaks truth to power, why is he called controversy? Why is he called a troublemaker? Why is he called a radical, a leftist, unamerican, a socialist, liberal, progressive?

A brother is called everything but a child of god. You hate me, and pull your sword.

I said it! We need peace in the Middle East. We need to stop feeding the beast. The military industrial complex … it's not complex. Free the land!

America has over 700 army bases around the world. Uncle Sam will rock your world. This is imperialism in your face. The American gangster, the world police, the world beast.

The global New World Order, the new world slaughter … no need to look at your watch, time is getting shorter - 2030.

Do you remember Al Gore? He is running around trying to save planet earth, but when he was in the White House he was killing people on planet earth.

Is that democracy or American hypocrisy? Climate change or climate game?

What about the Men in black? Who flooded the hood with crack? The CIA of criminals in America have a long history of murder, torture and kidnapping. But for some reason they are not considered a terrorist organization.

The Texas Rangers are no strangers. Old school country gang bangers. Kill the Redman, kill the Blackman, supporting slavery on Mexican land.

What about Baby Bush? A heavy drinker, a non thinker, I choked on my Pretzel. Mission unaccomplished, my Jokes are not funny. Mr. Water Board … Bush lied and thousands of Iraqis died.

What about the war on drugs? If America legalized drugs, the prison system would be empty. The war on drugs would be over. There will be no smoke stories about drug cartels bringing in cocaine, destroying American brains. You would not have to worry about the DEA or FBI kicking in your door at three O'clock in the morning looking for crack pipes.

Help me understand. Christopher Columbus killed more people than Hitler and we celebrate his birt day in America. What kind of party is that? The patriot act has successfully killed the constitution and free speech will send your ass to jail. Controversy! Controversy!

What is all this talk about controversy? No matter what I say or do, somebody is always calling me controversy.

Death Row / Life Row

You are indicted and charged with capital murder. The court appoints you an attorney because you are indigent.

You go to trial and the jury finds you guilty! Why because you were sitting in the wrong seat - the hot seat!

The jury finds you guilty of capital murder and sentences you to death row. You look over at your attorney and he is asleep! You are led out of the courtroom with a sad face, destination death row.

You come to death row and learn that people are actually being executed. Lots of people! The reality finally sets in - this is death row, death row, death row.

You are exhausted, stressed out and ready to drop your appeals. Until one day you hear a knock on your cell door and you look up and see a field minister.

God has heard your cry and has sent you an angel to bring peace to your heart. You accept this peace and slowly your life begins to change. People around you can see the change too!

And now you can proclaim to the world that you are on death row.

Digital Delights

The Internet is the tree of good and evil and its roots are global.

You can approach the internet and experience the good or you can experience the bad. Whatever you access is only a reflection of your nature - the truth in you!

Either way you will be rewarded.

The choice is yours.

Dylann Roof

American made white supremacist. He came to the Black church to prey on us, not to pray with us. If we had the fruit (F.O.I.) at the door he couldn't get us.

Genocide

Who will bring our case, our pain and suffering before the world body of the United Nations? Should it not be heard? After 500 long years of constant terror, slavery, rape, lynching, racism, police violence. Jim Crow, cross burnings, church bombings, and mass incarceration. Enough is enough! We the people charge genocide!

Reparations now!

Gentrification

You have never heard of this word until you and your family was on the curb homeless, forced to move out!

Gentrification is the name of the game coming to a Black community near you from the West coast to the East coast gentrification is a community killer.

Do you really need a Starbucks? Diversity development, so called nice words at the end of the day you find your ass on the curb.

A trojan horse gifted wrapped with a smile face. Slowly but surely taking your place, block by block. When will it stop?

How can we maintain the integrity of the Black Community without unity?

Green Justice

Have we learned anything about the trial of O.J. Simpson? We know that teamwork makes the dream work. O.J. was found not guilty, because he understood the color of justice.

Mail call

If commissary is necessary then mail call is the most important time of the day.

There is a stillness in the air when second shift arrives. I can hear an inmate scream: Mail call! Mail call!

Like a baby in a candy store grown men rush to their cell door hoping and praying for a piece of mail.

Big or small, one piece, two pieces, it really doesn't matter. The fact that someone from the free world is taking time to write us a warm letter is very therapeutic for a lonely incarcerated soul.

WRITE ME!

Publisher's note: Please check out the last page of this book. Thank you!

Monica

She lost her mind smoking water.
That's my cousin, my aunt's daughter.
One dip, two dip, she began to trip.
One more puff now she's stuck.
Her mind was chemically fried from the inside.
Do you know Monica?

My Soul

Can we get some recreation today?
No! I want to save your soul.

Are ya'll running showers today?
No! I want to save your soul.

My window is leaking, can you fix it?
No! I want to save your soul.

We have mold growing in the shower. Can you give the SSI bleach, so they can clean the showers properly?
No! I want to save your soul.

Can you give us some paint, so we can paint our cells?
No! I want to save your soul.

What can we have?
Tablets!!!!!

My Talking Knees

My knees have a tendency to talk when I walk. What do you expect? After twenty years of walking on concrete, my knees have started to speak out. What do they say you ask?

Snap, crack, pop.
Snap, crack, pop.

Every day they are talking and to my surprise, they have started communicating with other knees. Knees that are in worse shape than mine.

Snap, crack, pop.
Snap,crack, pop.

Knees that have been incarcerated over thirty years, grown men needing medical attention, shedding tears. What we need is some green grass on the bottom of our feet. At the end of the day, I need to get off this concrete.

Outcast

A father, brother and friend.
Funky Rob was his name.
But most people called him Big Foot!
He came from the east coast.
Seeking work down south but someone put a pipe in his mouth.
For thirty years he would smoke crack,
until his family came and took him back.
I miss him.

Political Pawn

Britney, I don't believe you went to Russia to smoke weed. You could have done that here. America is going green and up in smoke! You went to Russia to play basketball, won five champion ships and now they lock you up, for allegedly finding hash in your luggage. Who did that?

Reconstruction

Let's first start with freeing our minds,
so that our vision is clear.
We must build a bigger and better
Black Wall Street across America.
Our ancestors did it right after slavery
with little of nothing. We can do it.

Reform

They are up on the hill debating bills.
Supposedly taking care of the peoples' business.
Republicans and democrats alike.
Political theater checking for likes.
Politicians are the best actors.
They play their part well.
We need term limits.

Reparations

Over 400 years we have sung the Blues
Picked cotton and shined shoes.
How about that 40 acres and the mule?

San Quentin

My brothers are bruised, battle scarred but hard.
In the reck yard fighting hard.
You watch my back and the towers.

Slap!

Will Smith slapped Chris Rock!
Will Smith slapped Chris Rock!

And the whole world stopped.
Actors in Hollywood seem shocked.
Russia continues to drop bombs on Ukraine
and people tweeting and texting about Will's pain.

Solitary

Standing in the middle of the cell with arms stretched wide. I can touch each side. These walls are closing in, my friend …

Ask me how do I feel? Between four walls of concrete and steel … Talk to me!

Year after year, tear after tear. How much can a human being take before he breaks? Please talk to me!

Conversations mixed with salty tears. Unseen trauma building up, doing my best not to erupt … You better talk to me!

I'm in a deep depression, stressed out and ready to knock a mother fucker out!

Bad food equals bad moods. Bad food equals diabetes. Bad people, look at how they treat us!

Talk to me! Solitary confinement is torture!

Something Is Fishy

I am not anti vaccine
I am anti spike protein.
I don't want this poison
swimming in my blood stream.
Disrupting my natural immunity.
Causing harm and injury,
do you hear me?
But something is fishy.

I really would like for you to understand
I refuse to let them stick me.
I speak the truth … I know their history.
I read medical appartheid and cried,
I refuse to take that ride,
But something is fishy.

Listening to Fauci.
I know he's out to get me,
I am not paranoid - Just woke!
Trying to avoid blood clots and strokes.
No experiments for me.

This is a manmade disease
but they blame the Chinese,
fooling the world to raise up their sleeves.
A shot! A Jab! A booster!
Every six months they want to shoot you!
But something is fishy and you know it.

Spin Doctors

Around the clock, none stop, they won't stop!

The spin doctors are giving you news
that you can use, only on your cellphone.
Spindocors won't leave you alone.

Joe Biden and friends are at it again.
People are moving to the left.
People are moving to the right.
Mask on!
Mask off!
You want to fight?

Whipped into a frenzy the stress sets in
dividing family and friends.
The spin doctors have done it again
keeping the people divided.
Who needs the news?
Do your own home work, it won't hurt.

The Courtroom

The courtroom is an organized crime scene. A crying shame where people play games with your life. A circus with moving parts. A certified clown show without the funny. Lady Justice is blind folded and hogtied, tape across her mouth. What can she say?

Everybody and everything is moving like cloc work, coming in and out 9 to 5 and grown men crying. Who's next? A daily sick ritual I must say. You have to see it to believe it.

I was the main course on the menu of injustice. Not only was my zipcode wrong, I knew I was going down. I felt like I was in the twilight zone. The bailiff was playing with his gun and the prosecutor was breast feeding her baby. The judge was smiling at me holding a noose in his hand.

The courtroom is an organized crime scene. A cold heartless place, controlled by heartless people.

The Foreign Counter

The middle east, the far east and beyond.
Speaking in strange tongues.
They have come a long way.

Traveling over ten thousand miles,
with a wink and smile,
maybe with a parasitic agenda,
under cover, espionage tinted windows.

Setting up shop on every block.
Letting brothers hustle and sell rocks.
If the cops come I have a flash spot.

Foreign hands across foreign counters,
suspicious eyes all around us,
selling us crack pipes and K2,
Cigarettes dipped in crazy glue.

Weapons of Mass destruction,
purchased over the counter,
helping us in our destruction.

All along maintaining a smile on their face.
They have come from a foreign place.

The Talk

My daddy never had the talk with me.
Never knew anything about black history.
Never played football.
Never threw a pass to me.
Never took my hand and had the walk with me.
Never laced me up on being black in America.
Never said nothing … I think he was scared of her.
Never said anything about police brutality.
Never spoke on it … Slave mentality.
Growing up dumb I believed the police to be our friends.
There were no cameras, you couldn't see them sin.
My daddy never had THIS TALK with me.

He should have!

Urban Assault

They flooded the hood with crack.
Just to see how we would react.

From a distance they studied us like human lab rats. Taking copious notes as the whole hood went up in smoke. Pretending to be the lightman, the mailman, the gasman. Secretly moving among Black people with an unseen hand.

They flooded the hood with crack.
Just to see how we would react.

Creating a generation of crack babies and crack mamas. A generational curse with toxic trauma. Entire families were destroyed overnight. One hit from the crack pipe.

They flooded the hood with crack. Just to see how we would react.

Our city was under siege with "FREEZE MOTHERFUCKER". As pigs kicked in doors, slamming blacks on floors, a total disrespect for Black life. America had declared war on drugs, labeling all Black men as thugs.

They flooded the hood with crack.
Just to see how we would react.

What Privacy?

Will dumb people move into a smart city? Pay attention before you make that move, don't be fooled. Everything that glitters is not gold.

In the smart city - AI. Will be on you like white on rice? Watching your every move that ain't nice. Convenience is the new con!

4 Pieces

My heart broke in 4 pieces …
So much pain and agony …
Please God release me!

My heart broke in 4 pieces …
My therapist gave me a pen
to connect the 4 pieces.

My heart broke in 4 pieces …
Mother consoles me with
songs of sweet Jesus.

My heart broke in 4 pieces …
Afrikan ancestors pouring out
love vibrations inspire me.

My heart broke in 4 pieces …
Scattered by the wind of time,
my broken heart landed
in your healing hands
And you taught me
how to love again.

Hit List

The hit list was posted in the dayroom
the dates are set, are you ready to die?
Ok, starting with you!
Kill him, him, him, him and him.
Damn! He got a stay.
Start over … Kill him, him, him and him.
Damn! Hold up, he got away.
He hung himself last night.

Start over … kill him, him, him and him.
Damn! Dann came back,
it wasn't him.
Okay, who's next?
Kill him, him, him and … hold up!
What's going on?
He has mental illness
we can't kill crazy people - we used to.

Start over … kill him, him, him and ....
Hold up what's wrong?
We can't kill them.
Why not?
They are juveniles … Damn!
When will the killing stop?

I Remember

People are always asking me about my childhood. They want to know how I was raised up. You know I come from a pretty rough neighborhood and many people outside the ghetto are very curious as to what goes on the ‘hood. They ask questions like: Do you like school? Do you go to church? Do you like sports? Have you ever tried drugs? I always tell them; I remember growing up a young cat, 1973 to be exact. I grew up a confused kid, I never understood the things I did. Never had toys to play with, I was a ghetto child tearing up shit.

I remember the good times and the bad times. I remember standing with mama in the cheese and butterline. I remember saving lunch money to buy wine. I remember standing on the corner selling dimes. I remember the jackers, killers and dope dealers. I remember the pimps, players and hustlers. I remember slamming cadillac doors with pimps in the trunk. I remember the geekers, tweekers and thrill seekers. I remember the rats and roaches. I remember shooting dice on the broken down porches. I remember mama crying saying she can’t take it anymore.

I remember running from the PoPo, I remember playing Super Mario Brothers on my Nintendo.

I remember homeboys smoking premo, trying to be cool. I remember being introduced to the game of pool. I wasn't a shark, but played my part. I remember at the hobo flats, I worked the flats. I remember I caught me a mark and broke his heart. I was a poor kid, so I did what I did. I cut school and started cutting crack, I had a fat sack, imagine that. Not bragging or boasting, I am just telling you what was happening. (I remember.)

I remember 1988 when the game was great. I remember when money was everywhere, no need to hate. I remember the crack game, like Nino Brown. I was having things, I remember homies blowing big weed like Snoop Dogg. I remember hoggin' the block like boss hog. I remember going in and out of state with weight. I remember breakdancing on cardboard boxes. I remember breakdancing on cardboard. I remember hanging out at club Roxy. I remember the cool cup lady. I remember people from New Orleans callin' me baby.

If you'd like to get in touch with Pete please write to:

Pete Russell #999-443
Polunsky Unit
3872 FM 350 South
Livingston, Texas 77351
USA

Don't forget to leave your return address so he can write you back! You are not allowed to send anything other than letters on white paper and/or photos! Please do not use stickers, glue or anything similar, because Pete would not get those letters delivered!